The I Did That Cat

By P. L. Rainey
Illustrated by Zachary Noland

Copyright © 2021 by P.L. Rainey
Published by Ideas to Books
15 Lucky Lane
Morrilton, Arkansas 72110

Printed in the United States of America.
All rights reserved. No part of this publication
may be reproduced, stored in a retrieval system,
or transmitted in any form or by any means—
for example, electronic, photocopy and recording—
without the prior written permission of the publisher.
The only exception is brief quotation in printed reviews.

Paperback ISBN 978-0-9725092-7-5
eBook ISBN 978-0-9725092-8-2

THIS BOOK IS DEDICATED TO CAROLINE, BEN, TAYLOR, LUKE, MADDOX, EMILY, ELIZABETH, AND AMELIA

For Jay And Palmer,

Happy Reading!

Ms. Patty

I am a horse.

If I knock over my trough,
what should I do?

I am a cow.

If I break the fence,
what should I do?

I am a pig.

If I trip the farmer,
what should I do?

I am a chicken.

If I break an egg,
what should I do?

I am a dog.

If I chew up a boot,
what should I do?

I am a girl.

If I leave the gate open,
what should I do?

I am a boy.

If I break the tree swing,
what should I do?

I am a cat.

If I spill my milk,
what should I do?

What should they do?

Should the horse say,

"I just don't know who knocked over the trough"?

He should not do that!

Should the cow say,

"That was already done when I got here"?

She should not do that!

Should the pig say,

"That silly farmer just fell down"?

He should not do that!

Should the chicken say,

"Everyone else was pushing and playing and broke that egg—not me"?

She should not do that!

Should the dog say,

"That boot should not have been left outside"?

He should not do that!

Should the girl say,

"I didn't open the gate—
my brother did it"?

She should not do that!

Should the boy say,

"I didn't break that swing—
my sister did it"?

He should not do that!

No! No!

That's not what they should do!

Because those things

just are not true!

But . . .

when the question came
to the cat, he didn't lie.

He didn't blink.

He didn't ask,
"What do YOU think?"

He didn't blame

someone else or make up
excuses for his own mistake!

When the question came,

"Who spilled the milk?"
the honest answer came out straight!

He said,

"I am so sorry, but it was me."

"I am the cat

who just did that."

Made in the USA
Monee, IL
09 March 2021